GREAT RELIGIOUS LEADERS

Moses

and

Judaism

Sharon Barron

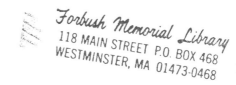

A+

Smart Apple Media

Great Religious Leaders

The Buddha and Buddhism   Jesus and Christianity
Guru Nanak and Sikhism   Muhammad ﷺ and Islam
Krishna and Hinduism   Moses and Judaism

First published by Hodder Wayland, 338 Euston Road, London NW1 3BH, United Kingdom
Hodder Wayland is an imprint of Hodder Children's Books, a division of Hodder Headline Limited.
This edition published under license from Hodder Children's Books.

Text copyright © 2002 White-Thomson Publishing Ltd
2/3 St. Andrew's Place, Lewes, E Sussex, BN7 1UP, UK

Edited by Margot Richardson, Designed by Jane Hawkins, Graphics and maps by Tim Mayer

Published in the United States by Smart Apple Media
1980 Lookout Drive, North Mankato, Minnesota 56003

Printed in Hong Kong

Library of Congress Cataloging-in-Publication Data

Barron, Sharon. Moses and Judaism / by Sharon Barron. p. cm.   (Great religious
leaders)
Includes index. Summary: An introduction to the religion of Judaism and to Moses, one of
its ancient prophets and leaders.
ISBN 1-58340-219-5
1. Moses (Biblical leader) Juvenile literature. 2. Judaism Juvenile literature. [1. Moses
(Biblical leader). 2. Judaism.] I. Title. II. Series.
BS580.M6 B264 2002   296 dc21   2002023140

9 8 7 6 5 4 3 2 1

Cover top: Moses descending from Mount Sinai, carrying the tablets of stone.
Cover main: Orthodox Jews with the Torah at the Western Wall, Jerusalem.
Title page: Orthodox Jews at a bar mitzvah at the Western Wall, Jerusalem.

Picture Acknowledgements: The publisher would like to thank the following for permission to reproduce their pictures:
AKG 7 (Erich Lessing), 8 (Cameraphoto), 9, 10, 11 both, 12, 13, 14, 15, 16, 18, 22, 23, 33, Art Directors and Trip Photo Library 5 (A Tovy), 26 (H Rogers), 27 (top) (H Rogers), 27 bottom (I Genut), 30 (I Genut), 31 (J Greenberg), 32 (K McLaren), 36 (top) (J Greenberg), 36 (bottom) (I Genut), 43 (A Tovy), 45 (A Tovy); James Davis Photography 29; Paul Doyle *title page*; Eye Ubiquitous 20 (David Peez), 42 (Chris Fairclough); Sonia Halliday 34 (David Silverman), 38 (both) (David Silverman), 29 (David Silverman); Impact 24 (Rachel Morton), 28 (Simon Shepheard); Christine Osborne 7 (top), 19 (Ann Cook), 25, 40; Panos Pictures 44 (N. Durrell-McKenna); David Silverman 35, 41; Stockmarket 37, 40; Hodder Wayland Picture Library 6, 17 (Rupert Horrox).

Contents

What Is Judaism?

Judaism is the religion of the Jewish people. The story of how it began is told in the early books of the Bible, which Jews call the Torah.

Early Judaism

The founding father of Judaism was Abraham, who lived approximately 4,000 years ago. Although he lived amongst people who worshipped many gods, Abraham believed that there was just one God. He was able to recognize God's voice and trusted Him when God told him to leave his home and go to a place called Canaan. God rewarded Abraham for his faith. He promised Abraham that he would become the father of a great nation and that he and his descendants would hold the land of Canaan forever. Canaan became known as "the Promised Land" and is in roughly the same area as present-day Israel.

The map below shows Canaan; the area in Egypt where the Israelites settled; and the route they took when they left Egypt to travel back to the Promised Land. ▼

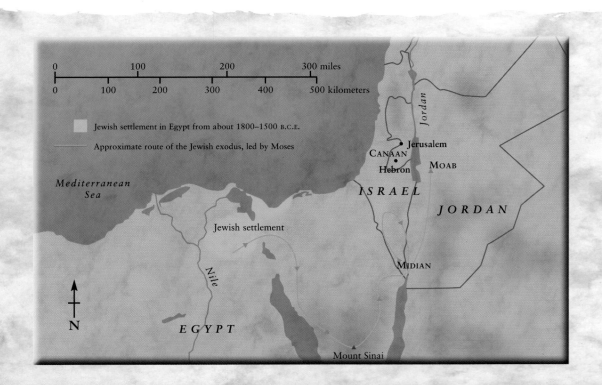

0   100   200   300 miles
0   100   200   300   400   500 kilometers

▢ Jewish settlement in Egypt from about 1800–1500 B.C.E.

— Approximate route of the Jewish exodus, led by Moses

Jerusalem
CANAAN
Hebron   MOAB
ISRAEL
JORDAN
Jordan

Mediterranean Sea

Jewish settlement

Nile

MIDIAN

N

EGYPT

Mount Sinai

The early Jews, who were called Hebrews, or later, Israelites, remained in Canaan for about 200 years, until a terrible famine forced them to leave. They travelled to Egypt, where food was more plentiful. At first they prospered in Egypt, but their good fortune did not last. An Egyptian ruler, called a pharaoh, made them slaves. They were slaves for more than 200 years, until God took pity on them and sent Moses to lead them to freedom.

What do Jews believe?

Jews believe that there is one all-powerful and unchanging God who is the creator of the universe.

Every morning and evening observant Jews will recite a special prayer called the *Shema*. If it is at all possible, they also recite the *Shema* before they die. The *Shema* sets out the most important Jewish beliefs and responsibilities. It reminds Jews of their duty to love God and to obey His commandments. They should take especial care to teach these to their children. The *Shema* ends by saying that it was God who rescued the Jews from slavery in Egypt.

▲ A traditional Jewish family at the Western Wall in Jerusalem (see page 30).

THE BEGINNING OF THE SHEMA

"Hear, O Israel! The LORD is our God, the LORD is one. You shall love the LORD your God with all your heart and with all your soul and with all your might. Take to heart these instructions with which I charge you this day. Impress them upon your children. Recite them when you are at home and when you are away, when you lie down and when you get up."

Deuteronomy 6: 4–8

The Life of Moses

The Israelite Baby

The Israelites became slaves in Egypt because a new pharaoh did not trust them. He thought that there were too many of them and worried that they might make trouble for him. So he made them work as slaves. Their work was back-breaking, and life was very cruel.

▲ The Israelites suffered greatly when they were slaves in Egypt.

However, Pharaoh was not yet satisfied. He ordered that all the Israelite baby boys should be killed as soon as they were born. Every Jewish mother prayed that she would give birth to a girl. Pharaoh ordered all Egyptians to look for Israelite baby boys and throw them straight into the river Nile.

One mother decided that she must save her baby. She had managed to keep him hidden for three months, but was scared that he would be discovered. So, in desperation, she found a basket, and smothered it in tar to make it watertight. She put her baby into the basket and hid it amongst the reeds that grew along the riverbank. She sent Miriam, her daughter, to watch over the baby from a distance.

Pharaoh's daughter liked to bathe in the river, and that day she passed the very spot where the baby was hidden. She noticed the basket and sent one of her slave girls to fetch it. When she looked inside she saw the most beautiful baby she had ever seen. She realized that he was an Israelite baby, but when he started to cry, she knew that she could not let him come to any harm.

Miriam approached the princess nervously. "If you are going to keep this baby, I could find you a good nurse," she offered. She ran home for her mother. So the Egyptian princess adopted Moses, and his real mother became his nurse.

An ancient Jewish tale says that God sent a plague of searing heat to Egypt, which affected the princess very badly. However, as soon as she touched the infant Moses, her ills miraculously disappeared. ▶

▲ An ancient wall painting shows us how the princess might have looked.

THE EGYPTIAN PRINCESS

We know little about the Egyptian princess, except that she was a kind-hearted woman who saved the baby. She must have been very brave to challenge Pharaoh's orders. In the Bible we are told that her name was Bithia. This means "Daughter of God," a suitable name for someone who acted so well. She called her adopted son Moses. The name comes from Egyptian and Hebrew words that mean "to draw out." Bithia chose it because she drew Moses out of the river.

The Burning Bush

Moses grew up in the royal court and became a prince of Egypt. However, one day he noticed an Egyptian beating an Israelite slave. Moses was so angry, he killed the Egyptian man. Moses was now in great trouble—and was a wanted man.

Moses fled to Midian, outside Egypt, only to become involved in more trouble. A group of men had attacked some girls who were tending a flock of sheep. Moses rescued the girls and was welcomed by their grateful family. He married one of the girls and settled in Midian. He was no longer a prince. Moses had become a humble shepherd and was very happy in his new life.

▲ This ancient mosaic from Italy shows Moses staring in amazement at the burning bush.

One day, while out with the sheep, Moses saw an incredible sight. There, on the open ground, miles from anywhere, he saw a burning bush. It blazed furiously but remained undamaged. Moses could not believe what he was seeing. A voice called to him from the bush and announced itself as the voice of God. Moses listened in absolute amazement as God instructed him to return to Egypt. He told Moses to tell Pharaoh to free the slaves, and to tell them that he was going to lead them out of Egypt and into the Promised Land.

Moses was horrified. "No one will take any notice of me. Pharaoh won't let the slaves go, and none of them will believe that I am telling them the truth!" he cried.

"Moses, what is in your hand?" asked God. Moses jumped back as the shepherd's crook that he had been holding changed into a slithering snake. "Catch hold of it, Moses, and see what happens." Moses grasped the snake by its tail and once again it was his shepherd's crook. "With this and other signs that I shall give you, you will be able to convince them all," said God.

But Moses was still unsure. "How can I?" he protested. "I get nervous and stutter when I have to speak to people."

God was getting more than a little angry with him. "I will send your brother, Aaron, with you as your spokesperson. That is enough now, Moses, the matter is settled."

▲ These illustrations come from a 14th-century *Hagadah* (see page 40). They show Moses at the burning bush (top left); his reunion with his brother, Aaron (top right); the two brothers meeting Pharaoh (bottom left); and trying to impress him with the magical powers given to them by God (bottom right).

A LEGEND ABOUT MOSES

Moses spent a long time chasing a stray lamb. He caught up with it when it stopped to drink from a stream. Moses said how sorry he was that he had not realized the lamb had been thirsty. He saw that the lamb was tired and carried it all the way back to the flock. God noticed Moses' kindness and the care he had taken over one stray lamb. He decided Moses was just the man to shepherd his own flock, the people of Israel.

Let My People Go!

Moses and Aaron met Pharaoh to ask for the slaves' release, but Pharaoh just laughed at them and ordered the slaves to work even harder.

Moses and Aaron went to Pharaoh again. They tried to dazzle him with the magic shepherd's crook, but he was not impressed. Their next meeting took place on the bank of the river Nile. Aaron held the crook over the water, and the river turned to blood. But Pharaoh's magicians were ready to match Moses and Aaron, trick for trick. They had to try again.

▲ God did not want Pharaoh to give in too easily. This allowed God to show his awesome powers by inflicting 10 devastating plagues. These pictures come from an 18th-century German *Hagadah*.

◄ The Israelites were told to slaughter a lamb, mark their doorposts with its blood, and roast and eat the meat. This night gave rise to the festival of *Pesach* (see pages 38–41).

God sent a plague of frogs to Egypt, and Pharaoh seemed about to give in, but at the very last minute, he changed his mind. God then sent a plague of lice. Pharaoh became more and more angry, but he would not give in. Swarms of insects followed the lice. A terrible disease killed off all the Egyptian livestock, but still Pharaoh would not free the slaves. God told Moses to throw handfuls of soot into the air. The dust from the soot settled all over the country and spread a plague of festering boils. Next came a shower of enormous hailstones that ruined Egypt's crops. The Egyptian people begged Pharaoh to give in. He refused, and swarms of locusts finished off any crops that the hail had missed. Then came three days and nights of total darkness. It seemed that nothing would weaken Pharaoh's will.

God told Moses to prepare the Israelites to move quickly. Moses ordered each family to slaughter a lamb and mark their doorposts with the lamb's blood. Behind the marked doors they were safe, but that night all first-born Egyptian sons died, and a grieving Pharaoh finally agreed to let the slaves leave.

Moses and the Israelites fled to the Sea of Reeds. Looking back, they saw that Pharaoh had changed his mind yet again, and that the Egyptians were chasing them. God ordered Moses to hold his arm out over the sea, and the waters parted miraculously to allow the Israelites to cross safely. The Egyptians attempted to follow. At a signal from Moses, the sea returned to normal, and all the Egyptians were drowned.

In the Wilderness

After crossing the Sea of Reeds, Moses and the Israelites travelled into the desert. After seven weeks, they arrived at the foot of Mount Sinai. God had summoned Moses to the mountain to receive the Ten Commandments on tablets of stone. Moses was away with God for 40 days and 40 nights, and the people became tired and anxious. Moses had left Aaron in charge, but he was not having an easy time. The people had begun to doubt that Moses would ever return.

Aaron was worried. He knew he had to do something to calm the people down. He wanted to give them something they could see, to give them faith. After much thought, he told the people to gather together all the gold jewelry that they could find. They came back with the precious metal, and Aaron had it melted down. He molded it into a gleaming, golden statue in the shape of a calf. The people forgot all about God and Moses because they believed Moses had abandoned them. Even though there was no logic to it, they decided to believe that the statue of the golden calf had rescued them from Egypt.

Aaron built an altar in front of the golden calf so that the Israelites could worship the statue. The following day, they had a celebration meal with singing and dancing. ▼

God could see all this. He raged at Moses that He would destroy these ungrateful people, but relented after Moses pleaded for them. He sent Moses back with the commandments written on tablets of stone.

When Moses saw the statue he became furious. He took the tablets of stone and hurled them to the ground. He ran at the calf and broke it into a million pieces. He ground the pieces into powder, mixed them with water, and made the faithless Israelites drink it. He dealt very harshly with all those who did not immediately repent. Some of the people had not taken part in the calf worship. Moses ordered them to kill all those who had worshipped the idol.

▲ Even though Moses had pleaded with God not to destroy the Israelites, about 3,000 people were killed because of their lack of faith.

AARON

Aaron was Moses' elder brother. He became the first High Priest of Israel and the founder of the priesthood. He has become known as a peace-loving man, and this may be why he gave in to the people and built the golden calf. Perhaps he believed that the project would stop the people from fighting each other, or that if sin took place, he—not the people—would be blamed. Aaron was much loved. When he died, "All the house of Israel bewailed Aaron 30 days." He died before reaching the Promised Land.

Moses the Leader, and His Teaching

What Do We Know about Moses?

Moses was brought up as an Egyptian prince, but we are told in the Torah that he was a very humble man. He had a stutter and was embarrassed to speak in public. He became a caring shepherd and would help immediately if he saw that someone was being badly treated.

Moses sometimes had a quick temper. When the Israelites were trekking through the desert, they needed freshwater desperately. God told Moses to gather the people together by a rock and to ask it for water. Instead of asking as he had been told, the anxious and angry Moses hit the rock twice with his staff. God punished Moses severely for his disobedience and for his lack of faith: Moses never got to step inside the Promised Land.

▲ By striking the rock, Moses made it look as though he had produced the water. Instead, he should have shown the people that this power came from God.

Moses was not a God-like figure. He was a man who took on extraordinary tasks and managed to do extraordinary things, but he made mistakes, and he had to pay for them. At the very end of his life, Moses was allowed to look over into the Promised Land, but he was not allowed to enter.

This illustration shows Moses and Aaron promising food to the hungry Israelites. It comes from a 14th-century French Bible. In this illustration, as in many others, Moses appears to have horns. This is entirely due to a mistake in the earliest translation of the Hebrew Bible into Latin. When Moses came down from Mount Sinai, he should have been described as radiant. The mistake in translation implied that he had grown horns.

Moses and God

When God first called him, Moses was afraid and hid his face. However, he recovered quickly and was able to voice his doubts about the mission to Egypt. When his first meeting with Pharaoh was unsuccessful, Moses complained to God that He had broken his promise to deliver the Israelites from slavery. When God threatened to destroy the people after they had built the golden calf, Moses pleaded with Him to change His mind.

How do Jewish people regard Moses?

Moses remains very special to Jewish people. They respect Moses because he was chosen by God to help them. Jewish people call Moses *Moshe Rabbenu*, which means "Moses, our teacher." This is because he brought the Torah from God and taught it to the waiting Israelites.

"Never again did there arise in Israel a prophet like Moses—whom the Lord singled out, face to face, for the various signs and portents that the Lord sent him to display in the land of Egypt, against Pharaoh and all his courtiers and his whole country, and for all the great might and awesome power that Moses displayed before all Israel."

Deuteronomy 34: 10–12

▲ Of all the prophets, it was Moses who was given the ultimate privilege of receiving God's laws on the tablets of stone.

Moses the Leader

Moses the prophet

Moses was one of many Jewish prophets. These were men and women chosen by God to speak for Him to try to persuade people to mend their ways.

All the prophets were good people, but Moses was special and was the most favored by God. When Moses' brother and sister, Aaron and Miriam, criticized him, God reminded them how very special Moses was:

> "Hear these My words: When a prophet of the LORD arises among you, I make myself known to him in a vision, I speak with him in a dream. Not so with My servant Moses: he is trusted throughout My household. With him I speak mouth to mouth, plainly and not in riddles, and he beholds the likeness of the LORD."

> Numbers 12: 6–8

The covenant

Moses was the link between God and the Israelite people. When God gave Moses the Ten Commandments on Mount Sinai, He made an agreement with Moses as the representative of the Jewish people. This agreement, known as a covenant, was made with all Jewish people, not just with those

The Jewish people keep the covenant alive today by obeying God's commandments. This family is keeping the commandment to remember the Sabbath day by walking to the synagogue for the morning service.

who were present at Mount Sinai at that time, but with all those from the generations to follow.

As His part of the agreement, God promised to take care of the Jewish people. In return, the Jewish people had to promise that they would obey God's commandments. Jews are sometimes called "the Chosen People." The Jews were not chosen by God because they were a large or powerful nation. They were chosen because they were willing to follow God's laws.

"Now then, if you will obey Me faithfully and keep My covenant, you shall be My treasured possession among all the peoples . . . you shall be to Me a kingdom of priests and a holy nation."

Exodus 19: 5–6

Moses, the Teacher

The Ten Commandments

Seven weeks after they had fled from Egypt, God ordered Moses to tell the people to get ready because he wanted to speak to them. Three days later, they saw that Mount Sinai was covered by thick smoke. The mountain trembled. There were great bursts of thunder and lightning and the constant blaring of air blown through a ram's horn. This dramatic build-up highlighted the importance of what was to come.

God called Moses to the top of the mountain and gave him the Ten Commandments. These orders, taken by Moses to the waiting Israelites, became the starting point for the whole of Jewish law and for legal systems all over the world.

THE TEN COMMANDMENTS

1. I am the Lord your God who brought you out of the land of Egypt.
2. You shall have no other gods beside Me.
3. You shall not swear falsely by the name of the Lord your God.
4. Remember the Sabbath day and keep it holy.
5. Honor your father and your mother.
6. You shall not murder.
7. You shall not commit adultery.
8. You shall not steal.
9. You shall not bear false witness against your neighbor.
10. You shall not covet your neighbor's house or anything that is your neighbor's.

Exodus 20: 2–14

▲ When God handed Moses the tablets of the law, He told him they were to be stored in an Ark made from wood and gold.

The 613 *mitzvot*

Although there were 10 main commandments, 613 commandments were given altogether. In Hebrew, the commandments are called *mitzvot*.

There are many *mitzvot* about food and its preparation. They detail which foods Jews may eat (kosher) and those that are not allowed. Another group of *mitzvot* deals with *tzedaka*: how Jews should help those in need. Helping others plays a large part in the life of any Jewish community.

Orthodox Jews follow the *mitzvot* as they are written and believe that doing this will strengthen their connection to God. They believe that the *mitzvot* are written in the words of God and must not be altered.

Modern followers of Judaism think that the *mitzvot* were written by men who were inspired by God. But, because they do not accept that the *mitzvot* are written in the actual words of God, they believe that they can be reinterpreted and adapted to a modern way of life.

▲ Hasidic Jews in Jerusalem, Israel. The Hasidic movement began in Poland in the 18th century, and its members are ultra-orthodox. They continue to dress in the Eastern European costume of their original leaders.

The Sacred Texts

The Tenakh

The Jewish Bible is called the *Tenakh*, and it has three parts: the Torah (the Five Books of Moses); *Nevi'im* (the books of the Prophets) and *Ketuvim* (the Writings).

The *Tenakh* gets its name from the first letters of the title of each of the three sections: TNK. The *Tenakh* is sometimes called the Written Law.

The Torah

The Five Books of Moses are the most important books of the *Tenakh* because they contain the laws of Judaism and because they tell the story of how Judaism began.

The Book of Genesis is about the creation of the world, Noah's flood, and the lives of the Patriarchs: Abraham, Isaac, and Jacob. Exodus tells how God guided Moses to rescue the people of Israel from Egypt and how they received God's holy law. Leviticus outlines many of the laws. In Numbers, Moses deals with uprisings and wars, and sets up a council of elders to help him lead the people.

◀ The Torah is so important that it is treated with great reverence.

The last of the five books, Deuteronomy, is Moses' farewell to the people. Before his death, Moses repeats the laws and teaching revealed in the first four books.

The Torah and the Bible

The Five Books of Moses are also part of the first section of the Bible, which is called the Old Testament. Jewish people do not use the term "Old Testament" because the second part of the Bible, the New Testament, is not part of Jewish scripture.

This father is teaching his son to read the Torah from a printed version called a *Chumash*. People use a *Chumash* for study purposes and for following the Torah reading in the synagogue. ▼

READING THE TORAH

The Five Books of Moses have been divided into 54 sections. Each of these sections is called a *sidra*. A *sidra* is read each week at the synagogue, during the Shabbat morning service, and on Monday and Thursday mornings. In the course of a year, each of the 54 sections will have been read.

Although Jewish people speak of "reading" from the Torah, the *sidra* is actually chanted rather than read. When the passage is finished, the Torah scroll is lifted up, and the congregation says in unison: "And this is the Torah, which Moses set before the children of Israel, according to the commandment of the Lord by the hand of Moses."

Nevi'im

The story of the Jewish people is continued in the books of the Early Prophets. After the death of Moses, Joshua (Moses' assistant) led the Jewish people across the river Jordan into Canaan, the Promised Land. A monarchy was set up, and the people were ruled by three powerful kings: Saul, David, and Solomon. After Solomon's death, the country was divided into the kingdoms of Judah and Israel.

The first book of the Later Prophets is the Book of Isaiah. This contains the famous prophecy of Isaiah: that one day everyone will live in peace and harmony, and there will be no more war.

▲ Before Moses died, he asked God to appoint a new leader. God instructed him to find Joshua and place his hand upon him. This action showed the transfer of leadership from Moses to Joshua.

A passage from Prophets, called the *haftarah,* is read aloud in the synagogue after the reading of the *sidra.*

Ketuvim

Ketuvim means "the writings." It is a collection of 14 different books. *Ketuvim* begins with the Book of Psalms. The Book of Psalms is a series of songs written in praise of God. There are 150 psalms in all, and it is thought that almost half of them could have been written by King David. Moses himself might even have written Psalm 90, which is headed "A prayer of Moses, the man of God." Psalms play an important part in synagogue services.

Many of the other books of *Ketuvim* continue the history of the Jews. Some of these books are read in the synagogue on specific festivals. The Book of Esther, the story of a brave Jewess who became a queen of Persia, is read on the festival of Purim.

When people tell the story of Jonah, they usually say that he was swallowed by a "whale." The Bible actually says that Jonah was swallowed by a big fish. ▼

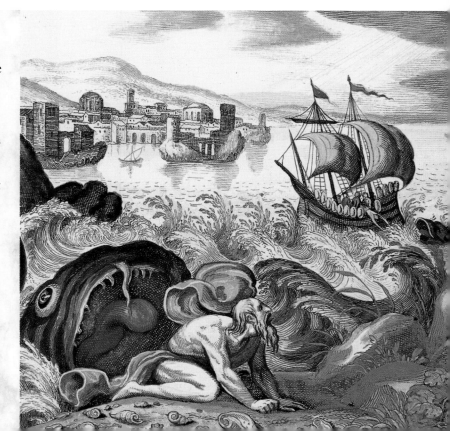

PROPHETS

God chose many men and women to become prophets and speak to the people on His behalf. This was not always an easy or a comfortable thing to do. A man called Jonah did not want to be a prophet at all. He ran away from the responsibility and was caught in a terrible storm at sea, thrown overboard, and swallowed, as the story goes, by a whale. Eventually, he came safely to the shore and carried out the task that God had set him. He went to the city of Nineveh and persuaded the people there to pray that God would forgive their wickedness.

The Writings of the Rabbis

The Talmud

The Talmud is a record of the studies of the early rabbis, who discussed how God's holy laws should be followed. The Talmud has two parts: the *Mishnah* and the *Gemara*.

The *Mishnah* and the *Gemara*

Mishnah means "to learn or to teach by repetition." The *Mishnah* was put together by Rabbi Judah the Prince at the beginning of the third century C.E. Jews were being forced from their homeland in large numbers, and Rabbi Judah recorded the discussions and rulings of the rabbis

THE RABBI

Rabbi means "my master" or "my teacher." The title of rabbi used to be given to anyone who knew a lot about Jewish law. Today, a rabbi has to complete an official course of study. Rabbis still spend a lot of time teaching and explaining points of Jewish law. They may lead the synagogue service, or a cantor or member of the congregation may do it. Women are able to become rabbis of non-Orthodox communities.

This rabbi works in a Reform (non-Orthodox) congregation. She carries out exactly the same duties as her male colleagues. There are no women rabbis in Orthodox Judaism. ▶

so that all Jews, wherever they lived, would follow the same traditions. The *Mishnah* covers the whole of Jewish law, from laws about land and crops to those that deal with cleanliness and the burial of the dead. The *Gemara* is a detailed discussion of the *Mishnah*.

The *Midrash*

The *Midrash* is a collection of writings by rabbis, many of them stories, that explain something in the *Tenakh*. This could be an event or a commandment. The word *midrash* means "enquiry." A famous *midrash* explains how Moses got his stutter.

When Moses was a small boy, his loyalty was tested by Pharaoh. A precious jewel and a pan of hot coals were placed together on a table, and Moses was led towards them. Pharaoh's advisors had told him that if Moses took the jewel, it would mean that one day he would try to take Pharaoh's throne. It would prove that Moses was not to be trusted and that he should be killed. Moses started to reach for the jewel, but an angel nudged his hand towards the pan of coals. Moses picked up a hot coal, touched his mouth with it, burnt his lips and tongue, and became "slow of speech and slow of tongue."

▲ Wherever they are, Jewish people will gather to study. This study session took place in Warsaw, Poland, during the Second World War. Early in the war, the Nazis herded 500,000 Jews into a ghetto and imprisoned them behind a high brick wall. Even as many were dying from starvation or diseases, religious study still took place.

Parchment Scrolls

Sefer Torah

In synagogues, the Torah is read from a scroll called the Sefer Torah. The Five Books of Moses that make up the Torah are the holiest of all Jewish scriptures, and a Sefer Torah is always treated with great care and respect. The Sefer Torah will have a beautiful velvet or wooden cover and other rich ornaments.

A Torah scroll is made from pieces of parchment that have been sewn together to form a single scroll that is about 200 feet (60 m) long. This long scroll is wrapped around wooden poles that have been attached to each end. The poles are used to unwind the scroll as it is being read. Whilst he or she is reading from the Torah, the reader will point to the words with a finger-shaped pointer called a *yad*. This is so the scroll is not touched unnecessarily.

The Torah is handwritten on the scroll in 250 vertical columns. This is slow and careful work, and a scroll will probably take as long as a year to make.

▲ The Sefer Torah is the most sacred of all Jewish objects. When the writing on the scroll has faded so much that it can no longer be read, the scroll is buried with great respect.

The scrolls are kept in the synagogue, in a special cupboard called the Ark. The congregation stands as a mark of respect whenever the Sefer Torah is taken from the Ark.

Mezuzah

Mezuzah is the Hebrew word for "doorjamb." It is the name given to a small piece of parchment that has the first two paragraphs of the *Shema* written on it (see page 5). This piece of parchment is rolled into a small, decorative container and fixed to the right-hand doorjambs of rooms in a Jewish home. It is a constant reminder of God's presence and commandments.

▲ The *mezuzah* is placed in its case and fixed in the upper third of a doorjamb.

Tefillin

Like the *mezuzah*, *tefillin* remind the wearer of God's commandments. *Tefillin* are two small black leather boxes with straps. The first two paragraphs of the *Shema* and two passages from Exodus are written on parchment scrolls in each of the boxes. Orthodox Jewish men wear *tefillin* while reciting their morning prayers. One of the boxes is worn on the center of his forehead and the other on his left arm.

▼ A Jewish boy will start to use *tefillin* during morning prayer after he has had his bar mitzvah (see pages 36–37). *Tefillin* are not used on Shabbat and festivals because it is thought that no further reminder of the covenant is needed.

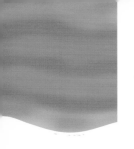

Sacred and Special Places

The Promised Land and the Holy City

The land of Israel has been at the heart of Judaism since the religion began. God promised Abraham the land of Canaan for himself and his descendants. Moses led the children of Israel back towards this Promised Land after the hardship of their time as slaves in Egypt.

▲ Much of Israel's fertile land is now used to grow many different kinds of fruit.

THE PROMISED LAND

"For the LORD your God is bringing you into a good land, a land with streams and springs and fountains issuing from plain and hill: a land of wheat and barley, of vines, figs and pomegranates, a land of olive trees and honey: a land where you may eat food without stint, where you will lack nothing. . . ."

Deuteronomy 8: 7–8

The land of Israel

Jewish people have not always had control over the land that is now called Israel, and for much of their history, many Jews have lived outside Israel. But Jewish writings and prayers show that they never forgot their Promised Land and always longed to return. Each time that Orthodox Jews recite a special prayer after they have eaten, they say: "And rebuild Jerusalem, the holy city, speedily and in our day."

Jerusalem

The holy city of Jerusalem was built on the site of a fortress captured by King David and is sometimes called the "City of David." David's son, Solomon, carried out his father's plan to build a temple there and made Jerusalem the capital of his kingdom. This temple (the First Temple) was destroyed in about 586 B.C.E., and the

Jews were forced into exile in Babylon. The Temple was later rebuilt (the Second Temple) and destroyed again, this time by the Romans in 70 C.E. Jews were expected to travel to Jerusalem three times a year to celebrate the festivals of *Pesach*, *Shavuot*, and *Sukkot* while the Temple was still standing. These three festivals are called Pilgrim Festivals. Jerusalem has very special importance for Christians and Muslims, as well as for Jews. Pilgrims of all these faiths travel to Jerusalem to visit their holy places.

Sacred Jewish, Muslim, and Christian buildings contribute to the special beauty of Jerusalem. The rabbis say that 10 measures of beauty came into the world, and that of these 10, Jerusalem took nine. ▼

Jewish Pilgrimage Sites in Israel

The Western Wall

All that remains of the First and Second Temples in Jerusalem today is a part of the wall that was built around the Temple Mount in the first century B.C.E. This is the most sacred Jewish site. For many centuries, Jewish people have come to the Wall to mourn the loss of the Temple. Because of the sound of their crying, it is sometimes called the Wailing Wall.

Today, a space has been cleared in front of the Wall for religious services. Bar and bat mitzvah ceremonies are often held there (see pages 36–37).

Visitors often write prayers on pieces of paper and push them between the gaps in the stones, in the hope that prayers sent from such a holy place will be answered favorably.

These boys are being taken to the Western Wall as part of their preparation for bar mitzvah (see page 36). ▼

Burial sites

There are many sacred burial sites in Israel and the surrounding area. The oldest and largest Jewish cemetery in the world is on the Mount of Olives in Jerusalem. Jews have been buried here for more than 2,000 years. This cemetery is the holiest of all burial sites for Jews.

The Tomb of King David is also in Jerusalem. It was built in the Middle Ages. It is unlikely that it marks David's real burial place, but it has become a site of pilgrimage and prayer. The Patriarchs—Abraham, Isaac, and Jacob—are thought to have been buried at the Cave of Machpelah in Hebron.

These sites, as well as the graves of many famous rabbis, are holy places where people come to pray to God. They sometimes leave written prayers at these holy places as they do at the Western Wall.

▲ The Mount of Olives used to be covered by olive trees. Instead of flowers, Jewish people place a small stone on a grave as a sign that they have visited.

THE DEATH OF MOSES

Rabbinical legend says that as Moses died, he was kissed by God. Moses has no known burial place.

"So Moses the servant of the LORD died there in the land of Moab, at the command of the LORD. He buried him in the valley of the land of Moab, near Beth-peor; and no one knows his burial place to this day."

Deuteronomy 34: 5–6

In the 1930s, the Jews of
Germany lost their freedom, just
as the Israelites had in Egypt so
many years before. But Adolf
Hitler, the leader of the German
Nazis, attempted to destroy the
Jews completely. The Nazis sent
Jews from all over Europe to
death camps. Six million Jews
had been killed by the end of the
Second World War. One-and-a-
half million of these were
children.

◀ The Children's Memorial at
Yad Vashem was hollowed out
from an underground cavern.

Places to Remember the Holocaust

Yad Vashem

Yad Vashem is Israel's memorial to those who died in the
Holocaust. It is a large complex built on the Mount of
Remembrance in Jerusalem, with exhibition halls, museums,
and special collections of art and information about the
Holocaust. The names of those who died are displayed
here, and there is a special and very sad memorial to all the
children who died. The memorial candles placed there are
reflected in the darkness and look like stars shining in a
dark sky.

The Anne Frank house

Before the Second World War, Anne Frank was a lively Jewish schoolgirl living in Amsterdam. When the Nazis invaded Holland, Anne and her family were in great danger. Her father made plans for them to hide in a secret apartment above his office. In 1942, with the help of trusted friends, the Frank family disappeared from view. They remained hidden for two years. They were betrayed in August 1944, captured by the Germans, and sent to a death camp. Anne died just two months before the end of the war.

Her father survived and after the war returned to Amsterdam, where he found Anne's diary. The diary was published, and Anne became famous. Today, her hiding place, the Secret Annex, is a museum. Thousands of people from all over the world, Jewish people especially, visit her former hiding place out of respect for her memory.

Memorial sites across the world

There are memorials to the Holocaust victims all over the world. The former death camp of Auschwitz-Birkenau (in Poland) has become a museum memorial to those who were murdered there, as have many of the other camps. There is the Holocaust Memorial Museum in Washington, D.C., and an underground memorial crypt in Paris. A museum in Copenhagen tells a happier story. It shows how most Danish Jews were helped to escape to safety in Sweden.

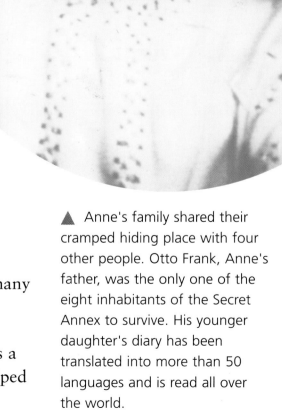

▲ Anne's family shared their cramped hiding place with four other people. Otto Frank, Anne's father, was the only one of the eight inhabitants of the Secret Annex to survive. His younger daughter's diary has been translated into more than 50 languages and is read all over the world.

Special Occasions and Festivals

Jewish people celebrate many festivals, spread out through the Jewish calendar. The Sabbath, or Shabbat, is a special day that is celebrated every week by Jewish families.

Shabbat

The Jewish Sabbath is called Shabbat. Shabbat is the only festival or special day mentioned specifically in the Ten Commandments. It is a day that is set apart from the rest of the week. When Jews rest and pray on Shabbat, they remember that God rested on the seventh day after He created the universe. They also remember that they have the freedom to rest on Shabbat because God rescued them from slavery. Shabbat begins just before sunset on a Friday evening and ends at nightfall on the following day.

Celebrating Shabbat

Friday evening is a time of celebration in a Jewish home. Orthodox Jews will not do anything that could be seen as work during Shabbat, such as switching on electricity or driving a car. Even families who do not follow all the customs will usually treat Friday evening differently and will gather together to enjoy a special meal.

In a traditional home, Shabbat begins when the woman of the house lights the Shabbat candles and

◀ The two Shabbat candles represent the two parts of the fourth commandment: to "remember" the Sabbath day and to "keep it holy."

recites the blessing. In a family with children, the father will bless his children, placing his hands over each child's head as he does so. Then it is time for the *Kiddush*, a blessing recited over a cup of wine, thanking God for the gift of Shabbat. A further blessing is made over two plaited loaves of bread called *challah*.

Many families attend synagogue services on Shabbat mornings. The high point of the morning service is when the Sefer Torah is taken from the Ark for the reading of the week's *sidra*.

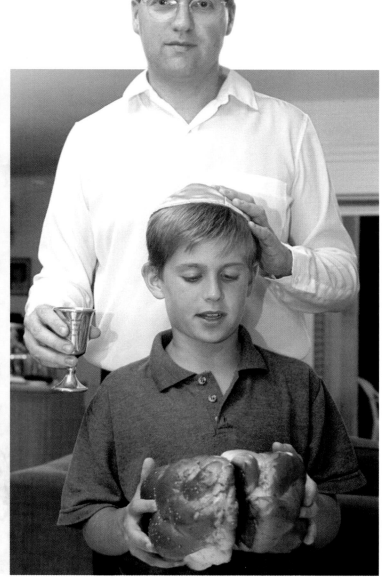

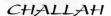

CHALLAH

Challah is a type of bread that is always served on Shabbat and festivals. There are two loaves on the table at Shabbat, as a reminder of the Israelites' desert trek. While they were in the desert, God gave them a food called manna, which was like "a wafer made with honey." On the sixth day of the week, God sent them a double portion. This gave them enough to eat on the sixth day and on the seventh, which was Shabbat.

The two loaves are held while the blessing is recited. At the end, everyone responds by saying, "Amen." The bread is then cut, and everyone is given a slice. ▶

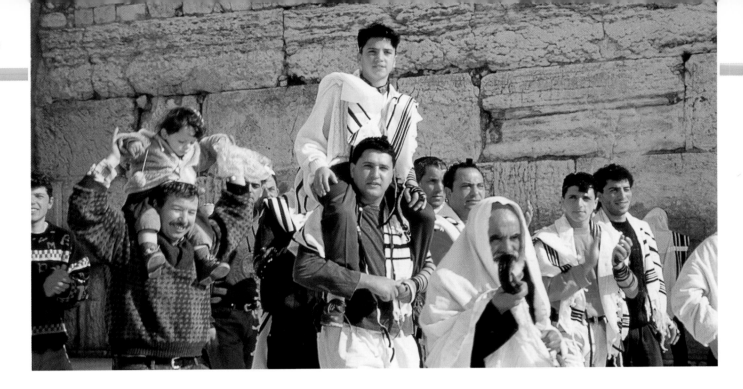

▲ A bar mitzvah at the Western Wall. The boy has completed his reading and has been lifted onto his father's shoulders as the family sings and dances in celebration.

A boy making a speech at the party that is being held to celebrate his bar mitzvah. He will pay tribute to his parents, grandparents, and teachers. ▼

Rites of Passage

Bar mitzvah

When a boy reaches the age of 13, he will celebrate his bar mitzvah. The ceremony usually takes place on the Shabbat that follows his 13th birthday. It marks the fact that, in the eyes of his religion, the boy has become a man. Bar mitzvah means "son of the commandment," and the boy should now observe all the Jewish laws. He can take his place as an official member of a *minyan*, the group of 10 men who must be gathered before a service can take place. The boy will now wear his *tefillin* for morning prayers.

During the synagogue service, the bar mitzvah boy will recite a blessing on the Torah. He will go on to read some or all of the *sidra* and sometimes the *haftarah* or other parts of the service as well. He will have studied very hard to get to this point.

A bar mitzvah is a time for great celebration. The proud parents will give a party, and the boy will receive many presents. His parents and grandparents will usually try to give gifts that he will keep always: a *tallit* (prayer shawl), *tefillin,* or his own *kiddush* cup.

Bat mitzvah

Bat mitzvah means "daughter of the commandment." Bat mitzvah ceremonies take place when a girl is 12. Twelve has always been the age when a Jewish girl is considered to have reached adulthood, but it has only become usual to mark this with a ceremony in recent years.

A girl will attend special classes for some time before a bat mitzvah and study the *mitzvot* and Jewish history. She will spend a lot of time learning how to run a Jewish home.

A bat mitzvah ceremony taking place in a non-Orthodox synagogue. It is held in the same way as a bar mitzvah. The girl is wearing a prayer shawl and is reading from a Sefer Torah. ▼

There is not really a set pattern to the ceremony, but it will always include the Torah passage that begins "A woman of worth who can find? For her price is beyond rubies" (Proverbs 31: 10–11) as a reading or a song.

Reform and Progressive branches of Judaism treat boys and girls in exactly the same way, and a bat mitzvah ceremony is held during the regular Shabbat morning service in these congregations.

Festivals

Pesach

This festival, also called Passover, takes place in spring and lasts for eight days. It is the festival of freedom, the time when the Jewish people remember the exodus from Egypt and thank God for releasing them from slavery. As Jewish people celebrate, they should feel as if they themselves had been rescued from Egypt and set free.

Hametz

On the night that Moses lead the Israelites out of Egypt, they made bread for their journey. They had to leave so quickly that there was no time to wait for the bread to rise. Jewish people remember this by avoiding *hametz* (leavened foods) during *Pesach*. They do not eat anything made from grain products that have risen or fermented and will eat matzah instead of bread at this time. Matzah is a flat, unleavened bread made from special flour and water, rather like a cracker or crispbread.

Matzah dough is baked within 18 minutes to make sure it will not have any time to rise. ▶

▲ Any last crumbs of *hametz* are gathered together and burnt before *Pesach*. As it burns, the head of the household recites a blessing.

Some utensils can be made kosher for use during *Pesach* by immersing them completely in boiling water. ▶

Cleaning for *Pesach*

Not only do Jewish people avoid eating leavened foods, but they also avoid using anything that might have come into contact with them. Every trace of leavened food has to be removed from the house before *Pesach*. The house is spring-cleaned very thoroughly. The dishes, cutlery, and kitchen equipment that is usually used is put away, and sets that are only ever used during *Pesach* are brought out instead.

Pesach cookery

Jewish families all have their favorite foods for *Pesach*. There are many delicious recipes for special cakes and cookies. Different communities have slightly different customs. Sephardi Jews (Jews from Spain, Portugal, and the Arab countries) continue to eat rice during *Pesach*. They also eat vegetables, such as peas or beans, that grow in pods. Ashkenazi Jews (Jews from Northern, Central, and Eastern Europe) do not eat these foods during *Pesach*.

SEARCHING FOR HAMETZ

However careful a family has been to remove all *hametz* from the house, they will search the house again on the evening before *Pesach*. This search is called *bedikat hametz*. Somebody will hide some pieces of bread around the house before the search begins. The search will not be over until all the pieces have been found. In this way the family can be absolutely sure that they have made a thorough search for every trace of the *hametz*.

What is Seder?

The Seder is the service and evening meal celebrated at home on the first two nights of *Pesach*. *Seder* means "order," and on Seder nights, everything is done in a particular and unchanging order. The service is divided into two parts by a special meal. Families gather together for the Seder and invite guests to join them who would otherwise be alone. Seder involves the whole family and is at the heart of the celebration of *Pesach*.

At the table

The Seder service is read from a book called a *Hagadah*. This means "telling." Many are brightly colored with beautiful illustrations. The youngest child at the table is

▲ A *Hagadah* illustration that goes with a traditional Seder song called "One Kid."

Three pieces of matzah are placed on the Seder table. The middle piece is broken into two, and half of it is used for the *Afikomen* (see page 41). After the traditional blessing, everyone is given some of the top matzah and the remaining middle half to eat. ▼

given the job of asking four questions about why the Seder night is different from all other nights. The answers to the questions are given in the "telling" of the story of how Moses was sent by God to lead the Israelites out of slavery in Egypt.

A Seder plate is placed on the table. It has a number of sections for special foods that also help to tell the story. Everyone must taste the *Haroset* (a mixture of apples, nuts, cinnamon, and sugar that is meant to look like the mortar that the Israelite slaves used in building) and the bitter herbs that represent the bitterness of slavery.

During the Seder, everyone will drink four cups of wine. (Children will have a tiny cup, or wine mixed with water.) Each cup of wine stands for one of the four promises that God made to the Israelites: "I will free you," "I will deliver you," "I will redeem you," and "I will take you to be my people." The Seder evening is long, but everyone enjoys the familiar songs that are sung at the end of the meal.

The Seder takes Jews back to a time when they suffered greatly, but by the end of the evening, they start to look forward to a time when everyone will enjoy peace and freedom. The Seder celebration ends with the cry "Next year in Jerusalem!"

▲ In some families, everyone will take turns reading aloud from the *Hagadah*.

THE AFIKOMEN

Afikomen means "dessert." It is the last piece of matzah that is eaten at the Seder. It stands for the last, hurried meal that the Israelites ate before they fled from Egypt. During the evening, a father hides the *Afikomen,* and the children will have to find it after dinner. The Seder cannot be finished until the *Afikomen* has been found and eaten. The finder gets a reward, as do all the other children who joined in the search!

Shavuot, Sukkot, and Simchat Torah

Shavuot

The two-day festival of *Shavuot*, "the Season of the Giving of Our Law," celebrates the giving of the Torah to Moses on Mount Sinai. The Ten Commandments are read in the synagogue on the first day. *Shavuot* comes seven weeks after *Pesach* and is sometimes called the "Feast of Weeks."

Sukkot is also the autumn harvest festival. The overhanging branches of the *sukkah* are decorated with autumn fruits, leaves, and fragrant plants. These remain in place throughout the festival. ▼

It is also a harvest festival because it marks the beginning of the summer wheat harvest. On *Shavuot*, it has become customary to eat dairy foods, especially cheesecake, to remember the promise of the "land of milk and honey."

Sukkot

Sukkot commemorates the protection of God during the time that the Jewish people were wandering in the desert. Observant families build a *sukkah* to use during this eight-day festival in memory of the shelters that the Jews had to build in the desert. A *sukkah* is a shelter or hut, with three or four sides. Its roof is covered with cut branches and left partly open to the sky. The family will eat and even sometimes sleep in the *sukkah*.

THE FOUR SPECIES

Four plants are used during prayer on *Sukkot*: the palm, myrtle, willow, and *etrog*. They are known as the Four Species. The palm branch, myrtle, and willow are wound together to form a bundle called a *lulav*. This is held in the right hand. An *etrog*, a yellow fruit that is rather like a lemon, is held in the left hand. At set times during the celebration, the *lulav* is waved in all directions to show that God is everywhere and that He showers His blessings from all sides.

▲ To worship during *Sukkot*, people try hard to find the freshest and most perfect plants available. The *lulav* has to be green, its ribs should still be tight, and it must come to a point at the top. The *etrog* must be yellow, and its skin should be blemish-free.

Simchat Torah

On *Simchat Torah*, "the Rejoicing of the Law," the annual cycle of Torah readings comes to an end with the last verses of the Book of Deuteronomy. The readings immediately begin again with the first verses of Genesis.

The festival shows the love that Jewish people have for God's law. *Simchat Torah* is celebrated with all the joy of a wedding, and the Torah readers on *Simchat Torah* are known as Bridegrooms of the Law. The Sefer Torah is carried around the synagogue, and sometimes outdoors, with much singing and dancing.

Judaism Today

Where Jews Live

There are approximately 15 million Jewish people today. They live in countries all over the world and come from different racial groups. They may be Ashkenazi (from Northern, Central, and Eastern Europe), Sephardi (from Spain, Portugal, and the Arab countries), Oriental (from ancient communities such as India and Yemen), or Beta Israel (from Ethiopia).

▲ Most of the ancient Jewish community of Ethiopia was rescued from persecution in the latter part of the 20th century.

The Jewish population of Europe fell dramatically during the Holocaust, when one-third of the world's Jewish population was killed, and the largest numbers of Jews now live in the United States and Israel.

The State of Israel

Jews had prayed for a return to their homeland ever since they were forced to leave it. In the 19th century, the Zionist movement was formed. Its aim was the re-establishment of a Jewish homeland. The State of Israel was founded in 1948, and after the horror of the Holocaust, a second exodus began.

Israel's "Law of Return" gives every Jew the right to live in Israel and to become an Israeli citizen. The most recent group of new citizens has come from the former Soviet Union. Israel today is home to Jews from all over the world: Europe, the United States, the Arab countries, Ethiopia, and beyond.

Jewish religious movements

There are now a number of Jewish religious movements. They fall into two main groups: Orthodox and non-Orthodox. Orthodox Jews follow traditional religious rules and customs. Some Orthodox Jews belong to Hasidic groups that are strictly observant. The Lubavitch group is one of the largest Hasidic groups. Lubavitch Jews run many education programs and try to encourage other Jews to become more observant.

There are different non-Orthodox movements in different countries. These groups are not quite the same, but, unlike some Orthodox Jews, they all share a belief that Judaism can be adapted to meet the needs of a changing world.

These Orthodox Jewish men are celebrating at the Western Wall. The area near the Wall is divided into two sections, according to Orthodox tradition, providing a space for women and a separate space for men. ▼

Moses and Judaism today

The Torah is the heart of Judaism. This is true for all branches of Judaism, Orthodox and non-Orthodox. All that is different is how they understand and explain it.

Moses has a special place in Judaism because he was its greatest prophet and the very first Torah teacher. When Moses came down from Mount Sinai and told the people about God's commandments, he began the traditions of Judaism that have continued for thousands of years to this day.

Glossary

Ark The cupboard in a synagogue in which the Torah scrolls are kept.

Bar mitzvah A ceremony that is held to welcome a Jewish boy into the adult community.

Bat mitzvah A ceremony that is held to welcome a Jewish girl into the adult community.

B.C.E. "Before the common era."

Cantor The person who leads the prayers during a service in a synagogue.

C.E. "Of the common era."

Commandment A rule or order given by God.

Covenant An agreement or contract, as in the agreement between God and the Israelites.

Exodus A mass departure of people.

Ghetto A part of a town where Jews were forced to live.

Hagadah The book read at the Seder. It tells the story of the Jews' escape from slavery in Egypt.

Hametz Leavened food forbidden during *Pesach*.

Hebrew The language of the Jewish Bible and the traditional language of Jewish prayer. A modern version of Hebrew is the language of Israel.

Holocaust The persecution and mass-murder of the Jews by the Nazis between 1933 and 1945.

Kiddush A blessing said over a cup of wine at the start of Shabbat and festival meals.

Kosher Food which Jews are allowed to eat.

Leavened Food that has fermented and risen.

Mitzvot Commandments. Sometimes used to mean "good deeds."

Observant Observing the rules of a religion.

Orthodox Judaism Traditional Judaism.

Patriarch The male head of a family or tribe. Abraham, Isaac, and Jacob are the Patriarchs of Judaism.

Pesach The festival which marks the escape of the Jews from slavery in Egypt.

Pharaoh A ruler of Ancient Egypt.

Pilgrim Someone who travels to a holy place for religious reasons.

Plague A large number of animals or insects, or a serious disease that causes great damage.

Prophet Someone who speaks for God and tells people what God wants.

Purim The festival that celebrates the time when Queen Esther saved the Jewish people at the time of King Xerxes II of Persia.

Rabbi A Jewish religious teacher and leader.

Reform Judaism A non-Orthodox Jewish movement that has made changes to old religious laws and customs to fit in with changing times.

Sefer Torah A handwritten Torah scroll.

Shabbat The Jewish Sabbath. It begins before sunset on Friday and ends at nightfall on Saturday.

Shema An important prayer and statement of belief.

Sidra A passage from the Torah read in the synagogue on Shabbat mornings.

Synagogue A building where Jewish people meet, pray, and study.

Talmud A collection of commentary and discussion, written by the early rabbis, known as the Oral Law.

Tefillin Two leather boxes containing passages from the Torah that Jewish men wear on their head and upper arm during morning prayer.

Tenakh The Jewish Bible.

Torah The Five Books of Moses, but can also mean the Jewish Bible or the whole of Jewish law and teaching.

Yad A finger-shaped pointer used when reading from a Sefer Torah in a synagogue.

Further Information

Read More

Drucker, Malka. *The Family Treasury of Jewish Holidays*. Boston: Little, Brown, 1994.

Goldin, Barbara Diamond. *Bat Mitzvah: A Jewish Girl's Coming of Age*. New York: Viking, 1995.

Goldin, Barbara Diamond. *The Passover Journey: A Seder Companion*. New York: Viking, 1994.

Langley, Myrtle. *Eyewitness: Religion*. London: Dorling Kindersley Publishing, 2000.

McFarlane, Marilyn. *Sacred Myths: Stories of World Religions*. Portland, Oreg.: Sibyl Publications, 1996.

Morrison, Martha, Stephen F. Brown, and Fay Carol Gates. *Judaism*. New York: Facts on File, 1991.

Sullivan, Lawrence Eugene. *The Religious Tradition of Judaism*. Philadelphia, Pa.: Chelsea House Publishers, 2001.

Wood, Angela. *Jewish Festivals*. Crystal Lake, Ill.: Heinemann Library, 1997.

Wood, Angela. *Jewish Synagogue*. Milwaukee, Wisc.: Gareth Stevens Publishing, 2000.

Internet Sites

About.com: Judaism
(Online resource providing a basic introduction to Judaism, including customs and rituals, a holiday calendar, recipes, and additional links to information on the Torah, Israel, and the Holocaust)
http://judaism.miningco.com

Akhlah: The Jewish Children's Learning Network
(Informative website featuring a book-by-book review of the Torah, festivals and holidays, various blessings, Hebrew language basics, biographies of Jewish heroes from the Torah, and a geographic look at Israel)
http://www.akhlah.com

Judaism 101
(Internet site focusing on the beliefs, people, language, scriptures, holidays, customs, and rituals associated with Judaism from an Orthodox viewpoint; information ranges from basic to advanced)
http://www.jewfaq.org

Index